Macbeth
Classroom Questions

A SCENE BY SCENE TEACHING GUIDE

Amy Farrell

SCENE BY SCENE
ENNISKERRY, IRELAND

Copyright © 2016 by Amy Farrell.

All rights reserved. No part of this publication may be reproduced, distributed or transmitted in any form or by any means, including photocopying, recording, or other electronic or mechanical methods, without the prior written permission of the publisher, except in the case of brief quotations embodied in critical reviews and certain other noncommercial uses permitted by copyright law.

Scene by Scene
11 Millfield, Enniskerry
Wicklow, Ireland.
www.scenebysceneguides.com

Macbeth Classroom Questions by Amy Farrell. —1st ed.
ISBN 978-1-910949-37-5

Contents

Act One, Scene One	1
Act One, Scene Two	3
Act One, Scene Three	5
Act One, Scene Four	8
Act One, Scene Five	10
Act One, Scene Six	12
Act One, Scene Seven	14
Act Two, Scene One	16
Act Two, Scene Two	18
Act Two, Scene Three	20
Act Two, Scene Four	22
Act Three, Scene One	24
Act Three, Scene Two	27
Act Three, Scene Three	29
Act Three, Scene Four	31
Act Three, Scene Five	34
Act Three, Scene Six	36
Act Four, Scene One	38
Act Four, Scene Two	41
Act Four, Scene Three	43
Act Five, Scene One	46
Act Five, Scene Two	48

Act Five, Scene Three	50
Act Five, Scene Four	52
Act Five, Scene Five	54
Act Five, Scene Six	56
Act Five, Scene Seven	58
Act Five, Scene Eight	60
Act Five, Scene Nine	62

Act One, Scene One

Points to Consider

Students tend to enjoy the supernatural aspect to this opening scene. Discuss what contemporary films/ television shows/ music videos this scene reminds students of.

A discussion of witches and their alleged powers can heighten interest in the action.

Questions

1. What is the mood in this scene?

2. What powers do the witches seem to have?

Act One, Scene Two

Points to Consider

The language used to describe Macbeth here is very significant as it establishes him as a worthy, loyal soldier.

The references to bloodshed and battle are worth noting. Students could consider how these descriptions might appeal to an audience and grab their attention.

The fate of the Thane of Cawdor is significant, as Macbeth is about to earn this traitor's title. Ironically, these descriptions will later apply to Macbeth himself.

Questions

1. How is Macbeth described in this scene?

2. What sort of imagery do you notice in this scene? How does it add to the scene?

3. How does King Duncan intend to punish the traitorous Thane of Cawdor?

Act One, Scene Three

Points to Consider

It is interesting to discuss whether or not your students would be as quick as Macbeth to trust the witches and believe their prophecies.

His possible motivation for believing them so readily is worth considering, as is the motivation of the weird sisters for revealing these prophecies.

From a stagecraft point of view, it is worth considering how students would arrange and stage this scene (consider lighting, costumes, props, sound and special effects, etc.)

Questions

1. How do you know that the power of the witches is very limited?

2. How does Macbeth react to the witches' greeting? Why does he behave like this, in your opinion?

3. What do the witches predict for Banquo?

4. "Would they had stayed!"
   Why does Macbeth wish the witches had stayed longer?

5. "The Thane of Cawdor lives; why do you dress me
   In borrowed robes?"
   Comment on the imagery in this line.

6. What does Macbeth's new title convince him of? What does this tell you about his character?

7. What conclusion does Macbeth jump to when he hears himself mentioned as the future King? What does this tell you about Macbeth?

8. "Give me your favour: my dull brain was wrought
   With things forgotten."
   What has Macbeth really been considering?

9. Do you think Macbeth values Banquo as a friend? Explain your point of view.

10. In this scene, did the witches merely make a prediction, or are they encouraging, tempting or manipulating Macbeth?

Act One, Scene Four

Points to Consider

Consider King Duncan's qualities. Does he appear to be a kindly and interested ruler? This will allow comparison later on, when Macbeth seizes the throne.

Macbeth's reaction to the news of Malcolm being named as heir is interesting. He views Malcolm as an obstacle and appears to be considering murder already. What does this reveal about his character? What does it reveal about his belief in the prophecies?

It can be interesting to discuss how students view Macbeth's character at this point.

Questions

1. What comment does Malcolm make about Cawdor's death?

2. How do you know that King Duncan thinks very highly of Macbeth?

3. Are you convinced that Macbeth really believes that, "our duties are to your throne and state, children and servants"?

4. What is significant about Duncan's statement that "We will establish our estate upon Our eldest, Malcolm"?

5. What is Macbeth planning when he says "Let not light see my black and deep desires"? How do you feel about this?

Act One, Scene Five

Points to Consider

It can be interesting to discuss students' first impressions of Lady Macbeth – in particular, her view of her husband, her response to the prophecy and her dabbling in the dark arts.

It is worth discussing the Macbeth marriage as it is presented in this scene. Consider the strength of their relationship and their ambition.

Students' response to the planned murder of King Duncan is worth discussing. It may be necessary to explain how kingship was viewed as a divine duty in Shakespeare's day and how regicide was considered a sinful and unnatural act.

Questions

1. Why does Lady Macbeth fear her husband will fail to become King?

2. Does her view of Macbeth match the character we have seen so far?

3. What does Lady Macbeth ask the "spirits that tend on mortal thoughts" to do to her?

4. What kind of relationship do Macbeth and his wife have?

5. What does Lady Macbeth mean by
"look like the innocent flower,
But be the serpent under't"?
What is your response to this?

Act One, Scene Six

Points to Consider

It is interesting to discuss students' views of King Duncan and Lady Macbeth in this scene. She is often criticised for her cruelty and insincerity, while he appears as a kindly, respectful king.

Questions

1. What kind of hostess is Lady Macbeth?

2. What are your impressions of Duncan?

Act One, Scene Seven

Points to Consider

Macbeth's indecision is significant here, as it prevents him from being a base, bloodthirsty character. His initial refusal to murder the king, "We will proceed no further in this business," shows his moral conscience.

Lady Macbeth's control over and manipulation of Macbeth is worth considering. Students tend to enjoy dissecting their relationship after this scene.

Questions

1. What is Macbeth considering as this scene begins?

2. What reasons does Macbeth give against murdering King Duncan?

3. What sort of King is Duncan, according to Macbeth?

4. What is Macbeth's only motive to go through with it, before his wife arrives?

5. Upon her arrival, what decision does Macbeth tell his wife he has come to?

6. How does Lady Macbeth manipulate her husband?

7. What is your impression of Lady Macbeth in this scene? Explain your opinion.

8. What plan does Lady Macbeth propose for murdering Duncan?

9. Who has the power in this marriage? What makes you say this?

10. Do you think Macbeth was easily swayed by his wife?

Act Two, Scene One

Points to Consider

Draw attention to the way in which atmosphere and tension are created in this scene, in particular with the references to darkness, witchcraft and the "dagger".

It can be interesting to assess how close Macbeth and Banquo appear at this time, considering what is to come.

From the point of view of charting Macbeth's character development/deterioration, it is worth considering his attitude to murdering Duncan at this point.

Questions

1. "There's husbandry in heaven;
   Their candles are all out."
   How does the darkness contribute to this scene?

2. Do Macbeth and Banquo seem very close in this scene, in your opinion? Why is this the case?

3. "Is this a dagger which I see toward me,
   The handle toward my hand?"
   What is significant about Macbeth's vision?

4. Is Macbeth happy to kill Duncan, in your opinion?

Act Two, Scene Two

Points to Consider

Consider Lady Macbeth's excuse for not doing the deed herself and what it suggests about her character.

It is worth discussing the reactions of both characters to their crime, and considering who is coping best with the situation.

Questions

1. What is happening offstage as this scene opens?

2. What reason does Lady Macbeth give for not carrying out this deed herself?

3. Do Macbeth and his wife appear as cold, ruthless killers in this scene? Explain your point of view.

4. What is Macbeth's reaction to what he has done?

5. What is Lady Macbeth's reaction to the night's events?

6. Who is the dominant character in this marriage? Explain your viewpoint.

7. How does the knocking at the gate add to the tension in this scene?

Act Two, Scene Three

Points to Consider

It is worthwhile to draw attention to the imagery in the porter's speech and how it contributes to the atmosphere in this scene.

It is beneficial to point out the unnatural and "unruly" events that have been taking place, as this encourages students to realise how unnatural and wrong the killing of the king is.

Macbeth's killing of the grooms is worth discussing. He committed this act instantly, without hesitation, despite the fact that he knows these men were innocent.

Sometimes students are surprised that Donalbain and Malcolm flee the castle. Their dangerous predicament may need to be explained.

Questions

1. What is significant about the porter's speech as he goes to open the door?
   What does it make the audience think about?

2. Why do you think Macbeth says so little to Lennox and Macduff when they arrive?

3. What is significant about Lennox's comment that "The night has been unruly…"?

4. How does Macduff react when he discovers Duncan's body?

5. Why doesn't Macduff tell Lady Macbeth what happened?
   What is your response to this?

6. How does Macbeth react to news of the king's murder?
   What is your response to this?

7. Are you shocked by Macbeth's killing of the grooms?
   What is your view on this?

8. How do Malcolm and Donalbain react?
   Do you think they are suspicious of Macbeth?

Act Two, Scene Four

Points to Consider

This short scene is interesting from an atmospheric point of view. It establishes the 'unnatural' acts that are taking place that emphasise the wrong that has been committed in the King's murder.

Students tend to enjoy discussing why suspicion hangs over Duncan's sons and whether they were right to flee.

Questions

1. How is the mood set in this scene?

2. How does the Old Man view Duncan's murder?

3. Who is Macduff suspicious of?

4. How does Macduff feel about Macbeth?

Act Three, Scene One

Points to Consider

Students tend to have strong opinions on Macbeth's planned murder of Banquo here. Some may view it as a worse affront than killing the king, as Macbeth now intends to turn on his peer and 'best friend'.

It is worth discussing Macbeth's motivation for killing his friend and what it says about the development and deterioration of his character. The excuses and reasons he gives his hired murderers are also worth considering in this regard.

Questions

1. What is Banquo thinking about as the scene opens?

2. How does Banquo respond to Macbeth when he is told he must attend a "solemn supper"?
   Are you surprised by this?

3. How does Macbeth compliment Banquo in this scene?

4. How does Macbeth find out details of Banquo's afternoon journey, without drawing attention to the fact that he wants this information?

5. Who are "our bloody cousins", and what rumour is Macbeth spreading about them?

6. "Our fears in Banquo stick deep".
   Why does Macbeth see Banquo as a threat?
   Is he right to do so, in your opinion?

7. "For Banquo's issue have I filed my mind;
   For them the gracious Duncan have I murdered"
   How is Macbeth feeling here?

8. Are there any contradictions in what Macbeth is saying, or in his way of thinking in this soliloquy?

9. How does Macbeth motivate these men to kill Banquo?

10. Are you surprised by Macbeth's devious scheme here? Explain your point of view.

11. Do the murderers strike you as blood-thirsty killers? Explain.

12. What excuse does Macbeth make for not killing Banquo himself?

13. Has Macbeth put a lot of thought into this plan for Banquo's death? Explain.

14. Has Macbeth's character deteriorated? Explain.

Act Three, Scene Two

Points to Consider

In this scene we see that Lady Macbeth, like her husband, is uneasy and has been brought no joy by the crime she has committed.

It is interesting that Macbeth conceals his plans for Banquo and Fleance's murders from his wife. This can be an interesting discussion point in the classroom.

Questions

1. Describe Lady Macbeth's state of mind as the scene opens.

2. How do you know that both Macbeth and Lady Macbeth are suffering because of what they have done?

3. Why does Macbeth want Lady Macbeth to pay special attention to Banquo at the feast, in your opinion?

4. "Be innocent of the knowledge, dearest chuck,
   Till thou applaud the deed…"
   Why does Macbeth keep his plan from his wife, in your opinion?

5. Comment on Macbeth's choice of imagery as the scene closes.

Act Three, Scene Three

Points to Consider

Macbeth's treachery in sending hired killers after Banquo is noteworthy here. Students often feel the killing of his friend is a brutal and savage betrayal, that erases any nobility Macbeth may have possessed. Both his motivation and the state of his character are worth discussing.

Questions

1. Why has Macbeth sent a third murderer?
   What does this say about his state of mind?

2. Banquo shouts "Fly, good Fleance, fly, fly, fly! Thou mayst revenge."
   What do his dying words tell us about Banquo?

3. "We have lost best half of our affair."
   What will this mean for Macbeth?

Act Three, Scene Four

Points to Consider

The atmosphere Macbeth creates in this scene is worth discussing. It appears that his lords are afraid to say anything to displease or anger him. Surely, his crimes would be clear from what he reveals when he views Banquo's ghost, yet none of his guests pass comment?

Students enjoy discussing how they would stage this scene and what lighting, costume, special effects etc. they would make use of. The supernatural aspects of the scene make it appealing.

Students enjoy discussing what the appearance of this apparition to Macbeth suggests.

Lady Macbeth attempts to protect Macbeth in this scene. This is the last time we will see her as a self-assured, confident figure, so it is worth noting how she appears here.

Questions

1. "Is he dispatched?"
   Did you expect Macbeth to speak so coldly about the murder of his friend?

2. "the worm that's fled
   Hath nature that in time will venom breed,
   No teeth for the present."
   Is Macbeth right to see Fleance as a future threat?

3. "Which of you have done this?"
   How does Macbeth give himself away when he sees Banquo's Ghost?
   What does this tell you about his state of mind?

4. How does Lady Macbeth try to cover up for her husband?

5. Does Lady Macbeth show sympathy or understanding towards Macbeth when he sees Banquo's Ghost?

6. "This is more strange
   Than such a murder is"
   What effect does seeing Banquo's Ghost have on Macbeth?

7. "Avaunt, and quit my sight, let the earth hide thee!"
   How must Macbeth's guests be reacting to his outbursts?

8. "Take any shape but that, and my firm nerves shall never tremble" (lines 102-103)
Comment on this line of Macbeth's.
Why is this vision, in particular, so abhorrent to him?

9. Is Lady Macbeth the same dominant, controlling character we first met?

10. What is the mood as this scene ends?

Act Three, Scene Five

Points to Consider

This scene reminds us of the scheming of the witches and how they are using Macbeth to their own ends.

It adds to the growing atmosphere as it reinforces our awareness of evil in the play.

Questions

1. How have the witches angered Hecate?

2. What is Hecate planning for Macbeth?

Act Three, Scene Six

Points to Consider

This short scene provides us with information of what is happening in Scotland and England. We realise that public opinion is against Macbeth and that he is viewed as a "tyrant".

We are also informed of Macduff's move against Macbeth, in seeking Malcolm in the English court.

Questions

1. What view does the Lord have of Macbeth's rule?

2. What is Macduff planning, according to the Lord?

3. What is Macbeth planning, according to the Lord?

4. How do Macbeth's subjects feel about his rule?

Act Four, Scene One

Points to Consider

Students tend to like the supernatural aspects of this scene and can generally explain very well how atmosphere and tension are created.

Macbeth makes demands of the witches here and seems almost fearless in their presence, something else to note from the point of view of character development.

It is worth taking time over the predictions the witches make and explaining their meaning fully, in order for students to fully appreciate their significance later on. Also, these prophecies feed Macbeth's feelings of invincibility.

His bloody intentions towards Macduff are also noteworthy. His conscience and nobility have vanished at this point, something students are usually quick to pick up on.

Questions

1. "Double, double toil and trouble
   Fire burn and cauldron bubble"
   What are the witches doing as this scene begins and how does it add to the atmosphere?

2. What significance do you notice in the witches' ingredients?

3. The Second Witch exclaims "Something wicked this way comes" as Macbeth enters. What effect does this have on you?

4. How does Macbeth seem when he arrives?

5. What does the First Apparition warn Macbeth about?

6. What does the Second Apparition tell Macbeth? What effect do you expect this to have on him?

7. What announcement does the Third Apparition make and how does Macbeth respond to this?

8. What form does each Apparition take?

9. "I will be satisfied." What does Macbeth demand to know?

10. What news does Lennox bring Macbeth?

11. Macbeth decides that
"The very firstlings of my heart shall be
The firstlings of my hand".
What act does he intend to commit?

12. Describe Macbeth's character, at this point.

Act Four, Scene Two

Points to Consider

Lady Macduff feels her husband has left her and her family in a very vulnerable position, something that proves to be very true. Students will have contrasting views on whether Macduff did the right thing by fleeing to England, or whether he has in fact let his family down.

In this scene we hear of the horrors of living under Macbeth's rule and view first-hand his cruelty towards innocents. This is significant from the point of view of Macbeth's ambition and the development of his character.

Questions

1. Lady Macduff accuses Macduff of not loving and protecting his family as he should,
"He loves us not; He wants the natural touch".
What impression does this give you of Macduff?

2. Ross says,
"But cruel are the times, when we are traitors
And do not know ourselves; when we hold rumour
From what we fear, yet know not what we fear."
What impression does this give you of life under Macbeth's rule?

3. In your opinion, what is the point of the conversation between Lady Macduff and her son?

4. How do you react to the Messenger's warnings to, "Be not found here; hence, with your little ones"?

5. How does the killing of young Macduff affect your view of Macbeth?

Act Four, Scene Three

Points to Consider

Students sometimes find Malcolm's 'trickery' here frustrating, as they find it difficult to grasp why he would cast slurs on his own character. It may be necessary to stress that he needs to determine Macduff's true motives before he can fully trust him. It is also significant that Macduff is willing to excuse every proposed vice, such is his desire for a saviour for Scotland.

In this scene we receive further information about the poor state of Scotland under Macbeth.

Students do not always sympathise with Macduff when he learns of his family's slaughter, as they feel that he left his family exposed to this kind of violence. If this is the case, it may be necessary to stress his loyalty to his country, and also his personal sadness over what has occurred.

Questions

1. What state is Scotland in, according to Macduff?

2. Why doesn't Malcolm trust Macduff?

3. How does Macduff react to Malcolm's distrust?

4. What does Malcolm have to say about "him that shall succeed"?
   What does this suggest about Malcolm's character?

5. How does Macduff attempt to ease Malcolm's fears?
   What is your reaction to this?

6. Why does Macduff cry "O Scotland, Scotland!" in line 100?

7. "my first false speaking
   Was this upon myself" (line 130-131)
   Why did Malcolm lie to Macduff?
   Why is he slow to trust him?

8. What is significant about the English King?
   Why do we learn of him?

9. What description of life in Scotland does Ross give the other men?
   What does this tell us about Macbeth's rule?

10. Why does Ross want Malcolm to return to Scotland?

11. "Your castle is surprised;
    your wife and babes
    Savagely slaughtered".
    What is your reaction to this news?

12. How does Macduff react to the news of his family's murder?
    What does this say about his character?

13. 'This scene marks a turning point in the play.'
    How might this statement be true?

Act Five, Scene One

Points to Consider

Students tend to enjoy this scene, and some will sympathise with Lady Macbeth as we see her crumble mentally before us. It is interesting to note the various manifestations of her guilt and how it affects her.

There is a marked contrast between Lady Macbeth here and in earlier scenes, so this scene is very significant from a character development/ deterioration point of view.

Questions

1. Why has the Doctor been called by the Lady-In-Waiting?

2. What stops the Lady-In-Waiting from telling the Doctor what Lady Macbeth said in her sleep?

3. "she has light by her continually, 'tis her command."
   Why do you think, does Lady Macbeth always have a light nearby?

4. "Out, damned spot! Out, I say!"
   What is the cause of Lady Macbeth's sleepwalking?

5. How does this scene add to the atmosphere of the play?

6. What is significant about Lady Macbeth repeatedly rubbing her hands together as if washing them?

7. "Look after her." Why does the Doctor want the Lady-In-Waiting to keep a close eye on Lady Macbeth?

8. Are you surprised by Lady Macbeth's disintegration? Explain your point of view.

9. Do you feel sorry for Lady Macbeth here? Explain your view.

48 • MACBETH SCENE BY SCENE

Act Five, Scene Two

Points to Consider

In this short scene we learn that the Scottish lords have defected to Malcolm's side.

This scene builds tension and prepares the audience for the conflict that is to follow.

Questions

1. What is taking place in this scene?

2. How do you know that support for Macbeth is declining?

3. What picture of Macbeth is created in this scene?

4. Comment on the imagery in this scene.

Act Five, Scene Three

Points to Consider

It can be interesting to discuss Macbeth as he is presented here. He appears defiant and fearless, and there is perhaps something admirable in his reckless confidence in the face of adversity. However, some may feel that he foolishly clings to the witches' prophecies, refusing to acknowledge the reality of his situation.

The way he speaks about Lady Macbeth is very important. He seems removed from her, their close bond seems to have suffered as a result of the events of the play. This is something students may criticise him for, especially as she appeared to suffer so wretchedly in her last scene.

Questions

1. Macbeth says,
   "Bring me no more reports; let them fly all:
   Till Birnam wood remove to Dunsinane
   I cannot taint with fear"
   Do you think Macbeth is right to feel so secure?

2. How would you describe Macbeth's state of mind in this scene?

3. What news does the servant bring?

4. Describe Macbeth's treatment of the servant.

5. "I'll fight, till from my bones my flesh be hacked."
   Despite all he has done, is there still something admirable in Macbeth's bravery, or is he simply a mad man, in your opinion?

6. Macbeth tells the Doctor to "Cure her of that." Does he remain the devoted husband from the earlier stages of the play?

7. How has Macbeth and Lady Macbeth's relationship changed over the course of the play?

Act Five, Scene Four

Points to Consider

The fulfilling of the 'Birnam wood' prophecy is important here. It tends to spark student interest in how the other prophecies may be fulfilled to bring about Macbeth's demise. In this way, this scene adds to the tension and adds to the supernatural element of the story.

Questions

1. How does Malcolm intend to conceal his troops?

2. What is the significance of this?

3. What does Malcolm say about Macbeth's force?

4. What outcome do you anticipate from this battle?

Act Five, Scene Five

Points to Consider

Macbeth appears brave and fearless as this scene opens, suggesting that there is still something noble remaining of his character.

Many students will feel that Macbeth's response to the news of his wife's death, "She should have died hereafter", is cold and unfeeling.

Her death forces him to contemplate the meaning and futility of life, and so we see a deeper, more philosophical side to his nature.

Macbeth treats the messenger with scorn when he brings news of the approach of Birnam Wood. He does not doubt the prophecy however, and rushes to meet his end on the battlefield.

Questions

1. "I have supped full with horrors."
   How have these "horrors" changed Macbeth, in your opinion?

2. "She should have died hereafter;
   There would have been a time for such a word."
   What is your reaction to Macbeth's response to this news?

3. In line 33 the messenger says
   "I looked toward Birnam, and anon methought
   The wood began to move."
   What is your reaction to this statement?
   What will this mean for Macbeth?

4. How do you view Macbeth's character and state of mind as the scene ends?

5. What is Macbeth fighting for at this point?

Act Five, Scene Six

Points to Consider

This short scene prepares the audience for the onslaught Macbeth is about to face.

Questions

1. Do you think Macbeth has any chance of beating Malcolm, Macduff and Siward?

Act Five, Scene Seven

Points to Consider

Macbeth realises he is cornered, but desperately clutches to the fact that one "born of woman" cannot harm him. He willingly slays Young Siward, still convinced of his own invincibility.

Macduff declares that he is seeking vengeance and justice for his murdered family, something that students tend to understand and approve of.

Questions

1. What thought does Macbeth clutch to as this scene opens?

2. Does Macbeth show remorse after killing Young Siward? Describe his reaction here.

3. Macduff says "I cannot strike at wretched kerns." What is significant about this?

Act Five, Scene Eight

Points to Consider

The dark and bloody imagery in this scene is very atmospheric.

Macbeth is reluctant to fight Macduff, suggesting he feels guilty for the crimes he has already committed against the man. Here we see perhaps a glimmer of his former noble self.

When Macbeth learns that Macduff was "from his mother's womb untimely ripp'd," he falters, but is prompted to do battle when Macduff accuses him of cowardice. He refuses to be taken prisoner, and in so doing, shows something of the bravery of his character. Because of the manner of his death, some students, even those who judged him harshly in earlier scenes, may look more kindly on the fallen tyrant.

Questions

1. "Of all men else I have avoided thee".
   Why has Macbeth avoided Macduff, in your opinion?

2. "I bear a charmed life, which must not yield
   To one of woman born."
   Describe Macbeth as he faces Macduff.

3. What fate awaits Macbeth if he yields and surrenders to Macduff? Do you admire Macbeth for fighting Macduff?

4. Is this a fitting end for Macbeth? Explain your point of view.

Act Five, Scene Nine

Points to Consider

The natural order and sense of justice in the play is restored when Malcolm is proclaimed King of Scotland.

Students may have differing views on Macbeth's and Lady Macbeth's characters by the end of the play. Similarly, they may have differing views on who is 'to blame' for the course of action Macbeth took – himself, his wife or the weird sisters. It can be interesting to discuss these views before studying notes and commentary, as these sources often colour students' opinions and make them less confident of their own ideas.

Questions

1. Describe the mood in Macbeth's castle.

2. Malcolm describes Macbeth and Lady Macbeth as "this dead butcher and his fiend-like queen". Is this entirely fair?

3. Do you like this ending? Explain your point of view.

4. Who was your favourite character? What did you like about them?

5. Which character did you dislike most? Explain why you disliked them.

6. How does the supernatural add to this story?

7. What does this play teach us about ambition?

8. Assess the relationship between Macbeth and Lady Macbeth. Were they a good match? Where did you see power shifting from one to the other?

9. What did you enjoy about this play? Explain your answer.

CLASSROOM QUESTIONS GUIDES

Short books of questions, designed to save teachers time and lead to rewarding classroom experiences.

www.SceneBySceneGuides.com
www.facebook.com/scenebyscene

www.ingramcontent.com/pod-product-compliance
Lightning Source LLC
Chambersburg PA
CBHW071320080526
44587CB00018B/3296